GLOBAL ISSUES

AIDS

Katie Dicker

WAYLAND

First published in 2008 by Wayland

Copyright © Wayland 2008

Wayland
338 Euston Road
London NW1 3BH

Wayland Australia
Level 17/207 Kent Street
Sydney NSW 2000

Senior Editor: Claire Shanahan
Designer: Phipps Design
Photo Researcher: Kath Kollberg
Proofreader and Indexer: Jo Kemp

British Library Cataloguing in Publication Data
Dicker, Katie
Aids. - (Global issues)
1. AIDS (Disease) - Juvenile literature
I. Title
362.1'969792

ISBN 978 0 7502 5436 6

African Pictures: Shuter and Shooter p5 and cover, Eric Miller p6, p16, p17; p12, Guy Stubbs p20. Corbis:
Wendy Stone p7, David Turnley p21, Andrew Brookes p27, Liu Haifeng/Xinhua Press p24, Polak Matthew
p36, Reuters p41, Gideon Mendel p33, Wyman IRA p34, Markus Moellenberg/zefa p43. Getty Images:
Hulton Archive p13, AFP p30. Reuters p4, p19, David Gray p22, p40, p42. Rex Features: Francis Dean p9,
Photoreporters Inc p14, Sipa Press p29, p32, Nils Jorgensen p37, p38. Science Photo Library: J.C Tessier,
Publiphoto Diffusion p8, Eye of Science p10. Simon Roberts p18. UNAIDS: G Pirozzi p25 and Cover, p28,
Y Shimizu p44.

The author and publisher would like to thank the following people and organisations for their help and
participation in this book:
Deborah Jack, Rachael Bruce, Lucy Stackpool-Moore, Rhon Reynolds, Paul Harker, Simon Roberts
(www.simoncroberts.com), The National AIDS Trust (www.nat.org.uk), African HIV Policy Network
(www.ahpn.org), Panos (www.panos.org), Terrence Higgins Trust (www.tht.org.uk), Health Protection
Agency (www.hpa.org.uk), Newspaperarchive.com (www.newspaperarchive.com).

Printed in China

Wayland is a division of Hachette Children's Books,
an Hachette Livre UK company.
www.hachettelivre.co.uk

Contents

Chapter 1

What is AIDS?

On 5 June 1981, the world woke up to news reports of a new disease affecting gay men in America. Five homosexual men in Los Angeles had contracted a rare form of pneumonia. And before long, it became clear that gay men were not the only people affected.

A mystery disease

This was the beginning of our fight against AIDS, a disease caused by the Human Immunodeficiency Virus (HIV). Soon, a group of gay men in New York and San Francisco were found to have a new type of skin cancer, too. And when drug users

Today, HIV is found worldwide. We are all at risk – whatever age, gender or colour of skin – and we must learn about ways to protect ourselves.

began to show similar symptoms, doctors realised the disease was spreading.

More than 25 years have passed and, despite huge advances in medical science, AIDS is now one of the most destructive diseases in history. Over 25 million people have died from AIDS since 1981, affecting nearly every country worldwide. This mystery disease affecting a few homosexual men in America has developed into the worst pandemic the world has ever faced.

What is AIDS?

During the 1980s, tests revealed that HIV – a virus that weakens the immune system – was responsible for the mystery illness. The disease was defined by the Centers for

June 1981 A mystery disease is detected in California and New York, USA >>> **September 1982** The disease is defined as Acquired Immune Deficiency Syndrome (AIDS) >>>

Disease Control and Prevention (CDC) in the USA in 1982 and became known as AIDS (Acquired Immune Deficiency Syndrome). AIDS is a collection of rare illnesses that people with HIV can develop because their immune system is unable to fight against infection. But having HIV does not necessarily mean that you have AIDS.

AIDS is a fatal disease in many parts of the world. But new treatments and greater awareness are giving hope to people living with HIV.

often dependent on someone's general health and their access to healthcare. However, new treatments mean that today most people living with HIV do not go on to develop AIDS.

What are the symptoms?

The symptoms of AIDS vary, but include fever, diarrhoea, weight loss, swollen glands, or more serious infections and tumours. It can take years for HIV to damage the immune system so much that a person becomes unwell. But once someone has contracted AIDS, the average survival time is about a year. These estimates vary widely however, and are

How do you get HIV?

HIV is spread by the exchange of infected body fluids – mainly through sexual activity or from the exchange of contaminated blood. Although HIV is most common in sub-Saharan Africa, nearly every country in the world is now affected. With increasing levels of HIV infection, everyone needs to take precautions to protect themselves.

 December 1983 In the USA, the number of infections reaches 3,064, and deaths from the disease total 1,292 >>>

Is there a cure?

There is currently no cure for AIDS, but treatments can slow the speed at which HIV damages the body, to prevent AIDS developing. If someone is diagnosed early, and responds well to treatment, they can lead a full and active life – with normal life expectancy.

Treatment development

Research over the past 25 years has enabled scientists to understand more about the causes of HIV and the way the virus spreads. In the 1990s, the introduction of antiretroviral treatments brought hope to millions of people living with HIV. But it's a lifelong commitment: treatments have to be taken regularly; the drugs are very strong; and they can have unpleasant side effects. Recent developments, such as trials for an HIV vaccine and the introduction of microbicides, hope to revolutionise HIV treatment and prevention for future generations.

Women wait patiently for treatment at an AIDS clinic in Africa. Although antiretroviral treatments are now available, access is limited in many parts of the world.

Disease destruction

Nevertheless, until effective treatments are available for all, the impact of AIDS is having a devastating effect. Families are losing loved ones, children are becoming orphans at a young age, and the financial impact of the disease is forcing many communities into poverty. These repercussions are affecting countries and continents, too. Health services are under strain, skilled workers are dying, and research into prevention and a possible cure is costing billions of pounds.

 April 1984 Margaret Heckler, the US Health and Human Services Secretary, announces the isolation of the virus which causes AIDS and claims a test could be available within six months and a vaccine within two years >>>

Why is HIV spreading?

HIV does not spread easily. Using a condom during sex and avoiding contact with infected blood are two simple preventative measures. The virus is also unable to survive outside the body for more than a few minutes. So why are more people becoming infected with HIV? The past 25 years have taught us that many political and social influences are affecting the crisis, too. Today, we travel around the world more than ever before, some people have more sexual partners, and despite the warnings, many people remain complacent about how easily they may get affected. In some countries, there is limited access to treatment. In others, problems of adherence are causing different strains of the virus to emerge. Stigma around HIV is also preventing people from getting tested, increasing the risk of the virus spreading.

QUOTE >

In the 1980s, fears about the cause of AIDS were very real. Princess Diana made headlines when she went to open the UK's first specialist AIDS hospital ward in 1987.

'She shook my hand without her gloves on. That proves you can't get AIDS from normal social contact.'

A patient quoted in the Bureau of Hygiene & Tropical Diseases 'AIDS Newsletter', 10 April 1987.

Although AIDS has been in the news for over 25 years, it has taken time for public health messages to get through. Straight Talk *is produced in Uganda to address issues of sex education for adolescents – one specialist publication that is proving effective.*

 March 1987 The US Food and Drug Administration (FDA) approves azidothymidine (AZT) as the first antiretroviral drug for HIV >>>

January 1995 The CDC announces that AIDS has become the leading cause of death among Americans aged 25–44 >>>

Chapter 2

The History of AIDS

AIDS is not the first epidemic we have had to face. Major diseases of the past have also claimed millions of lives, devastating families, communities and countries. But AIDS has brought a different challenge. While we struggle to contain the disease, we also know that – with the right precautions – future infections could be prevented.

Deadly epidemics

Less than a hundred years ago, the Spanish flu (1918–1919) is thought to have taken over 50 million lives. In the 14th century, the Black Death killed around 25 million people. And more recently, in 2003, SARS and bird flu caused major scares around the world. Killer diseases are still at large and we are never free from risk. But with improving standards of healthcare, we are beginning to overcome the threat of most serious epidemics.

But the challenge of AIDS is different. It's not a contagious disease and in theory should be easily overcome – unlike other diseases, HIV is not passed through the air, spread through dirty water or transmitted by insects. But still, the threat is growing. What makes AIDS different from epidemics of the past is the range of political and social factors influencing its treatment and prevention.

Some deadly diseases are difficult to control. Malaria is spread from the bite of infected female mosquitoes. The virus remains a killer because it constantly adapts to treatment.

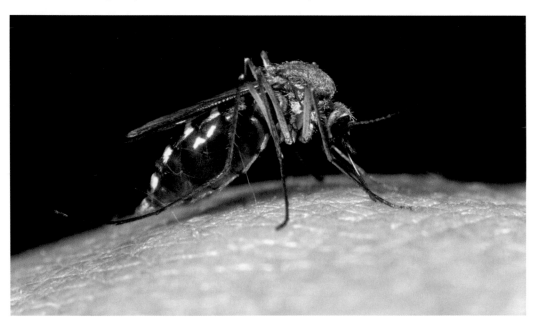

 May 1969 An African-American teenager, named Robert, dies from a mystery illness, later confirmed as the first case of AIDS in the USA >>>

April 1976 Arvid Noe, a Norwegian sailor, and his wife and two-year-old child, die from a mystery illness which is later linked to AIDS >>>

In the modern world, it is not uncommon for people to travel to different countries – to take holidays, or to live and work. This brings a greater risk of catching diseases – and HIV is no exception.

The early years

Although AIDS was first reported in 1981, examples of HIV infection have now been identified as early as the 1960s. Scientists believe that HIV was transferred to humans in central Africa around 1930, when infected chimpanzees were slaughtered for meat. When a person with HIV then travelled to Haiti in the 1960s, the virus spread, and soon it reached the USA, too.

Although HIV was unheard of at the time, tests on tissue samples have now revealed that the virus was the cause of mystery deaths in the 1960s and 70s.

In 1969, for example, a teenager from St Louis, USA, died from a rare form of cancer, and in 1976, a cancerous illness claimed the life of a Norwegian sailor. Doctors suspect he became infected with HIV in Cameroon, Africa, in the 1960s.

A growing concern

AIDS has now claimed over 25 million lives. What began as a localised problem in Africa, Haiti and the USA, has now spread to the far reaches of the globe. In 2007 alone, there were over 2 million deaths from AIDS and 2.5 million new HIV infections. What is even more worrying is that statistics do not tell the whole story. Scientists estimate, for example, that there are currently over 75,000 people living with HIV in the UK, a third of whom are undiagnosed.

 1999 Researchers at the University of Alabama claim that a chimpanzee, once common in West Central Africa, is the source of HIV >>>

Case Study: Dr James Curran, task force co-ordinator for the CDC

On 4 June 1981, the Centers for Disease Control (CDC) published a paper in *Morbidity and Mortality Weekly Report* (MMWR) about cases of Pneumocystis carinii pneumonia (PCP) in five homosexual men in Los Angeles, USA. This was the first published work to draw the world's attention to the as yet unknown disease called AIDS.

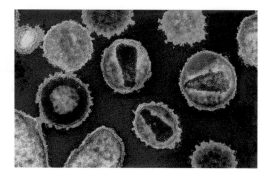

A coloured electron microscope image of a selection of Human Immunodeficiency Viruses (HIV) – the cause of AIDS. HIV attacks white blood cells in the body's immune system.

Urgent investigations

One month later, Dr James Curran was appointed the co-ordinator of the CDC 'Task Force on Kaposi's Sarcoma and Opportunistic Infections.' For 15 years, he directed a team of researchers investigating the cause and nature of the disease and the most effective ways to protect people from infection.

Before long, newspapers began to report initial findings about the curious condition. Because so little was known about the disease, there were worries that it was contagious, or could be spread by people who had no apparent symptoms. Doctors were puzzled – Kaposi's Sarcoma (KS) was a cancer usually found in older people and, until that time, PCP was a rare lung infection.

Piecing the jigsaw together

The cause of the disease was unknown and there was no evidence to suggest it was contagious. And for the time being, the condition seemed to only affect homosexual men.

Speculation about the reasons why a homosexual lifestyle could cause such severe symptoms began to surface. Nearly all the men first affected were frequent users of recreational drugs called nitrite inhalants (or 'poppers'). Some researchers thought this might be the key to the sporadic outbreaks.

But knowledge about the disease was changing fast – just five months later, in December 1981, PCP was found to affect a group of injecting drug users, and the condition was also reported in the UK. Researchers realised they had a long battle ahead.

> **July 1982** 23 states in the USA report a total of 452 cases of AIDS to the CDC >>> | **July 1982** There are reports of AIDS in Haitians, leading to speculation that the disease may have originated in Haiti >>>

WHAT THE WORLD THINKS...

These are four different publications commenting on the CDC's efforts in the 1980s. Compare and contrast the various viewpoints and see if you can find any more newspaper reports or other media discussing first documented cases of AIDS.

Michael S. Gottlieb, MMWR report, 4 June 1981

'The patients did not know each other and had no known common contacts...who had had similar diseases...Two of the 5 reported having frequent homosexual contacts with various partners. All 5 reported using inhalant drugs...'

Michael S. Gottlieb is the former assistant professor of medicine at the University of California, Los Angeles School of Medicine.

Pacific Stars and Stripes, 8 June 1981

'A parasite-caused pneumonia that killed two previously healthy men and infected three others may be linked to "some aspect of a homosexual lifestyle", [the CDC reports]. "The fact that these patients were all homosexuals suggests an association between some aspect of a homosexual lifestyle or disease acquired through sexual contact".'

Pacific Stars and Stripes is a newspaper published for the US Armed Forces overseas. This extract comes from an edition published in Tokyo, Japan.

Dr James Curran, CDC teleconference, 5 May 2006

'It is sometimes difficult to reflect 25 years, going back to five cases of pneumocystis in gay men in June of 1981, to understand how something that began so slowly and so quietly, can now be the number four cause of death in the entire world, something that we thought was a small problem back then...I think we still have to consider that we may be underestimating the burden and impact of this insidious [subtley yet harmfully spreading] global epidemic...'

The Gettysburg Times, 10 December 1981

'The condition – so new it does not have a name – has been reported in 180 people in 15 states...and 73 of the victims have died. "It is a very serious problem and does not seem to be on the wane," said Dr James Curran of the [CDC]. "This is probably just the tip of the iceberg."'

December 1982 The CDC reports the first cases of HIV passing from mother to child >>>

Chapter 3

AIDS Uncovered

We now know more about the origins of HIV and we've come to understand how the virus spreads. But scientists and social researchers are still baffled by increasing levels of infection. HIV prevention may look easy on paper, but in practice too many lives are still at risk.

Two strains of HIV have been identified, known as HIV-1 (from the Central Common Chimpanzee) and HIV-2 (from the Sooty Mangabey monkey).

The origins of HIV

Scientists now believe that HIV originated from human contact with chimpanzees and monkeys in Africa. Tests have revealed cases of a similar virus called Simian Immunodeficiency Virus (SIV) affecting these primates. SIV mutated to a human form, causing the symptoms of AIDS to develop in humans. But scientists have yet to discover why SIV-infected animals have not developed symptoms of this kind.

Local problems

Although HIV is a worldwide problem, the way the virus spreads in each country often varies. In Ukraine, for example, drug users were the first to be affected. The initial outbreak in the USA and the UK was largely limited to homosexual and bisexual relations, while in sub-Saharan Africa, heterosexual relations have been vulnerable to infection from the beginning. Today, with the spread of the virus reaching pandemic proportions, the disease is no longer confined to any particular group of society.

Unprotected sex

Despite variations between countries, the main cause of HIV transmission worldwide is unprotected sex. The use of a condom – while not 100 per cent effective – is a universal method of prevention. In the West, condoms are widely available and in most cases, unprotected sex is a choice. But, in other countries, access to condoms is limited. The use of contraception has clashed with religious beliefs and culture, too. Many African communities, for example, oppose the use of condoms.

July 1982 There are reports of AIDS affecting haemophiliacs >>>

November 1988 The US begins its first official syringe exchange program to protect drug users from HIV >>>

The Catholic Church has also long opposed the use of contraception. But in recent years, talks between the World Health Organisation (WHO) and the Vatican are bringing hope that barrier contraception will be supported in the fight against HIV.

Blood protection

In the 1980s, blood transfusions transmitted HIV in some cases. Today, in most countries, donated blood is tested and heat-treated to protect patients from the virus and medical staff wear latex gloves as a routine measure. Sterilised needles are now also offered to drug users, and recommended for practices such as tattoos and body piercing, to prevent the virus spreading via contaminated needles.

HIV can also be passed from a mother to child, during the last stages of pregnancy, at childbirth or while breastfeeding. Mothers with HIV can now reduce this risk, however, by using antiretroviral drugs during pregnancy, by having a Caesarean birth, and by bottle-feeding their child.

Most of the 2 million children living with HIV in sub-Saharan Africa became infected from their mother during pregnancy or through breastfeeding.

 1994 A large European study shows that Caesarean births halve the rate of HIV transmission between mother and child >>>

Case Study: The Ray brothers, HIV-positive from contaminated blood

In 1986, a family from Arcadia, Florida, was at the centre of a national controversy in the USA when the DeSoto County School Board banned their sons from attending classes because they had HIV.

Fear in the community

Ricky, Robert and Randy Ray contracted HIV through blood products used to treat their haemophilia. They were diagnosed in 1986 at 7, 8 and 9 years of age. When the family were ostracised by the local community, they moved to Alabama. But when school records were transferred, the boys were banned from their classes in Alabama, too.

The family moved back to Arcadia to fight their cause. They sued the DeSoto County School Board and in August 1987, won the right for the boys to attend school. But the discrimination continued. A local group called Citizens Against AIDS in Schools urged parents to keep their children at home. Bomb threats forced the temporary closure of the boys' school, Memorial Elementary, and a week after the court decision, the Ray's home was burnt down. Police suspected arson, but the case was never proved.

Raising awareness

In 1988, the family moved to Sarasota and began to campaign for greater awareness and understanding of HIV and AIDS. They spoke to groups across the USA and appeared on national radio and television shows.

In 1992, Ricky died – he was 15. But the family's continued activism saw the Ricky Ray Relief Fund Act passed in 1998. This law allows the US government to compensate haemophiliacs who contracted HIV between 1982 and 1987. Robert died in 2000, aged 22. Randy has been successfully controlling his symptoms using modern treatments.

Ricky and Robert Ray lost their lives because of contaminated blood used to treat their haemophilia. But their legacy lives on.

October 1985 All blood transfusion centres in the UK begin routine testing of blood donations for HIV >>>

28 August 1987 The Ray's family home is set alight. No one is prosecuted >>>

WHAT THE WORLD THINKS...

These are three different publications commenting on the Ray brothers. Compare and contrast the various viewpoints and see if you can find any more newspaper reports or other media discussing the Ray family and their impact on AIDS education.

Facts on File News Services website, 4 September 1987

'The fire capped a week of bomb and death threats against the Ray family, and a boycott of local schools. The boycott had been prompted by the Aug. 24 return to school of the three boys after a year's absence.

Louise Ray said that her family would leave DeSoto County. "I never thought it would go this far," she said.

The family's plight...attracted national attention, and offers of aid were pouring in from across the country. A family spokesman... indicated that the Rays wanted any donations from DeSoto County to go toward efforts to educate the community about AIDS.'

Miami Herald, 14 December 1992

'AIDS-infected Florida teenager Ricky Ray...died peacefully Sunday at his Orlando home. He was 15.

His family will continue his efforts to educate others about AIDS and fight for a cure, Louise Ray said. Her son had "wanted people to understand AIDS is not just this word that happens to somebody else – it can happen to everybody."

"Things changed so much for us around the country after the Ray family. People saw that education is really an imperative in dealing with AIDS," said Alan Brownstein, executive director of the National Hemophilia Foundation in New York. "They went through hell, but their hell has helped others."'

St. Petersburg Times, 2 September 2001

'Louise Ray had an epiphany the other day. She was visiting with a cousin here...and they were chatting about someone in town who is HIV-positive. They didn't speak in hushed tones or worried voices.

"And I thought, 'Boy, have things changed,'" she says. "You couldn't have had that conversation 10, 15 years ago. Now, as a general rule, having HIV has become more acceptable. You're not considered a leper to be cast away anymore."

1989 The UK government announces it will pay £42 million compensation to haemophiliacs who have been infected with HIV from contaminated blood products >>>

1993 Tennis star Arthur Ashe dies from AIDS. It is thought he contracted HIV from a blood transfusion in 1983 >>>

HIV antibody testing

When a person is tested for HIV, a small blood sample is usually taken from a vein in the arm. The test measures the amount of CD4+ T cells in the blood – antibodies caused by the body's response to HIV. When a person becomes infected, it can take up to three months for the antibodies to develop. If a person has contracted the virus, we say they are HIV-positive (but this actually means they are HIV antibody-positive).

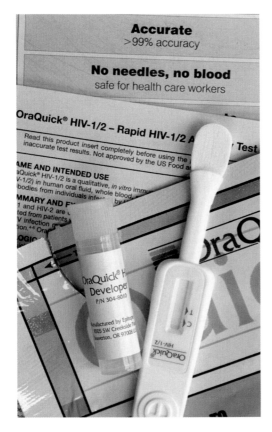

HIV tests measuring antibodies in a patient's urine or oral fluid are now available. They are often used in home-testing kits because they don't require the use of needles.

Treatment

Today, treatments for HIV can control the virus and delay the onset of AIDS in most cases. Highly active antiretroviral therapy (or HAART) was introduced in 1996. This usually involves a combination of three or more treatments – the drugs cannot kill HIV completely, but they help to stop the virus spreading in the body.

Antiretroviral drugs have to be taken regularly, as prescribed, to be effective. If a dose is missed, there is less medication in the body and a risk that the virus will reproduce. Different strains of the virus that are resistant to treatment may also develop, meaning another combination of treatments has to be tried. New treatments are being developed all the time, but the nature of the virus is also changing.

PEP treatments

If someone thinks they have been exposed to HIV, Post Exposure Prophylaxis (PEP) can reduce the likelihood of the virus attacking the body. This treatment was first introduced in 1996, for healthcare workers coming into contact with HIV-infected blood. The use of PEP is controversial, but the treatment may become more widely available in future. The drugs have to be taken within 72 hours of suspected infection and continued for four weeks. There are also side effects, such as headaches, fatigue, diarrhoea and vomiting, and a risk of liver or kidney damage in the long term.

June 1998 A Post Exposure Prophylaxis (PEP) programme begins in San Francisco, USA, to treat people who have recently been infected with HIV >>>

July 1998 The first case of HIV resistance to antiretroviral drugs is reported in San Francisco, USA >>>

Antiretroviral treatments are now improving the lives of many people living with HIV.

A vaccine for HIV?

Vaccinations encourage the immune system to create resistance to a virus. A safe and effective vaccine would hold the key to stemming the spread of HIV, with the potential to save millions of lives. It would potentially cost less than current treatments and would also overcome problems of adherence. But a vaccine is proving difficult to find. One difficulty is that HIV attacks the immune system – the very thing that

a vaccine is trying to activate. The nature of the virus is also constantly changing, making it difficult to find treatments that remain effective.

> QUOTE >
>
> 'HIV is one of the toughest viruses we have yet battled. The only thing that will beat it is the human brain.'
>
> **Dennis Burton**, professor at the US Scripps Research Institute, 2004.

 1999 The UK government announces pregnant women will be offered an HIV test to reduce the number of babies infected with HIV >>>

Chapter 4

The Impact of AIDS

When someone is diagnosed with HIV, they are not the only ones whose life changes. The virus is, of course, most serious to the health of the individual concerned, but the repercussions on friends and family – and even countries – can also be huge.

Human costs

Imagine being told that you have a serious virus, and that, unless you take medication for the rest of your life, you are at risk of developing a deadly disease. Imagine trying to share this news with your friends and relatives, with a prospective employer, or with a partner at the start of a new relationship. It can't be easy. But this is the reality for over 33 million people currently living with HIV.

A diagnosis of HIV can cause some people to feel isolated. Others face discrimination or are at risk of losing their income. At its worst, HIV can lead to a loss of life. Every death to AIDS is one too many, and the effects are also devastating for those left behind. In Less Economically Developed Countries (LEDCs) in particular, the death of a parent brings financial insecurity and the increasing number of children orphaned by AIDS – currently 12 million in Africa, for example – is a major concern.

An HIV-patient – Shimmer Gunda (aged 26) – lies in a church hospital in Zimbabwe. The effects of HIV are fatal for many people living in Less Economically Developed Countries.

Economic impact

Billions of pounds have been invested in the race to prevent HIV from spreading. It's an undeniably worthwhile cause, but it comes at a hefty price. In 2004, economists predicted an investment of US$27 billion could prevent around 30 million new HIV infections by 2010 – but what of the 33 million people already infected? Many countries, such as the UK, have committed to providing access to HIV prevention, treatment, care and support by 2010.

2001 India is reported to have the largest number of AIDS orphans in the world – 1.2 million >>>

2002 The number of children orphaned by AIDS reaches 13.4 million >>>

In sub-Saharan Africa, it is estimated that 9 per cent of children have lost at least one of their parents to AIDS.

But if HIV infections continue to increase at the current rate, this will not be affordable.

In countries that have a fragile economic base, deaths from AIDS can slow economic growth still further. The pandemic puts pressure on healthcare resources and workers may need time off to care for their loved ones. Skilled workers may be lost to the disease – and if tax revenues are cut, other services such as education and healthcare come under further strain.

> **QUOTE >**
>
> 'AIDS destroys families, decimates communities and, particularly in the poorest areas of the world, threatens to destabilize the social, cultural, and economic fabric of entire nations.'
>
> **Rabbi David Saperstein**, Director of the Religious Action Center of Reform Judaism.

 2002 Botswana becomes the first African country to provide free antiretroviral treatment. The programme is expected to cost US$24.5 million in the first year >>>

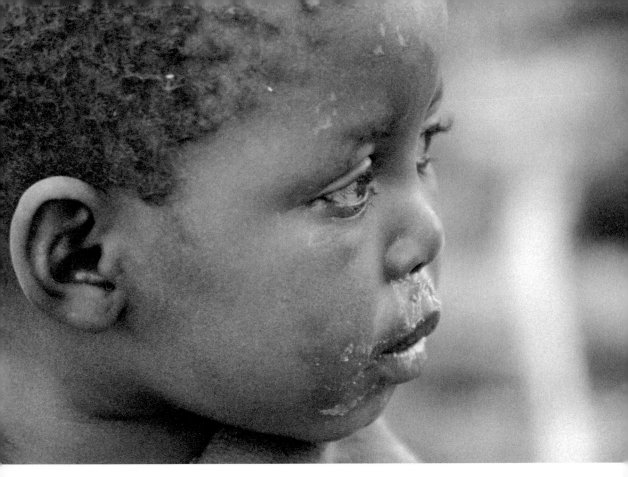

Stigma

HIV is not a visible condition and many people living with the virus find it difficult to talk about the disease. When someone is first diagnosed, there are real fears about job security, the reaction of partners and friends, and quality of life in the future.

Stigma creates the ideal conditions for HIV to spread. If someone with HIV avoids being tested or seeking advice about their sexual health, they risk passing the disease on to someone else. Stigma is fuelled by fear and ignorance and education is therefore vital to prevent misunderstandings and discrimination against those affected.

In some countries in Africa, children with HIV are denied access to schooling or healthcare. Children who have lost their parents to AIDS may also be wrongly-assumed to have HIV themselves.

Types of discrimination

In some countries, medical staff have refused treatment to people with HIV. Elsewhere, insurance policies have required a compulsory HIV test, and gay men have been refused health and life insurance regardless of their HIV status. Landlords have evicted HIV-positive tenants from their homes, and teachers and pupils have been dismissed from school because of an irrational fear they might transmit HIV to others.

 1985 Ryan White, a 13-year-old American haemophiliac with HIV, is banned from school >>> | **May 1988** The US government distributes 107 million copies of a booklet called 'Understanding AIDS' as part of a new education campaign >>>

Anti-discrimination laws, such as the Disability Discrimination Act 2005 in the UK, are helping cases of this kind, but sometimes they are not interpreted correctly. The stigma of HIV also reaches beyond those living with the condition – family, friends and carers can be a target, too.

Reinforced prejudice

The stigma surrounding HIV is often linked to other types of discrimination, such as racism or homophobia. In some countries, the gay or black community is an easy target for misinformed views. Inaccurate and biased media reports of HIV have enhanced this situation. Stigma is also apparent in what is not said – in the stories that don't get reported, because there are other, more grabbing headlines to feature.

Women's rights

In 2006, almost 60 per cent of adults living with HIV in sub-Saharan Africa were women. Studies have revealed that attitudes towards women is one factor causing HIV to spread. Some women are at risk of sexual assault or physical abuse if they disclose their HIV status. They may also have limited access to education, making them more vulnerable to infection. Condom use is not widespread in many African nations, and women are often unable to insist on barrier protection. Female condoms give greater control, but availability is limited and their cost can be prohibitive, particularly to those living in LEDCs.

While the world unites in the fight against AIDS, the disease is also associated with stigma and discrimination. Those living with HIV can feel marginalised by society.

QUOTE >

'What do I care for a disease that may kill me in 5–10 years when I know I won't have anything to eat tomorrow if I insist on condom use with my client?'

Sangita, 14, commercial sex worker, India, as quoted in UNDP's Regional Human Development Report, 2003.

May 1996 The US Food and Drug Administration (FDA) approves the first 'home sampling' tests for HIV >>>

Case Study: Margaret Marabe, an AIDS campaigner in Papua New Guinea

In August 2007, Margaret Marabe spoke to reporters in Papua New Guinea, claiming she had seen AIDS patients being buried alive. Margaret was a campaigner working for Igat Hope [I've Got Hope], a volunteer organisation. She had spent five months raising awareness of HIV and AIDS in the remote southern highlands of Papua New Guinea, a country in the eastern half of the Pacific island of New Guinea.

Women and children living with HIV secure refuge at a safe-house in Papua New Guinea because their lives are in danger.

Lack of awareness

Margaret claimed that poorly-educated families turned to such desperate measures because they could no longer look after their relatives and were terrified of being infected. She stressed the importance of extending AIDS awareness programmes to rural areas, where ignorance of the disease was widespread.

Speculation about the basis of these stories mounted. Some attributed the tale to a lack of understanding in rural communities, where 'victims' were marginalised and had no hope of accessing treatment. Others thought the reports revealed cultural practices in a region where euthanasia was unacceptable. There was also talk of a culture that regarded people with AIDS as the victims of witchcraft.

A growing crisis

Margaret's claims supported the United Nations' (UN's) reports warning that Papua New Guinea was facing an AIDS catastrophe. Officials claimed the mix of cultures and languages in the country was making it difficult to convey important public health messages.

In September 2007, an official investigation declared that Marabe's claims were unfounded. But the fact remains that the stigma of HIV is still very real after more than 25 years. And Papua New Guinea is not the only country affected. Growing suicide rates among those affected by HIV in India, for example, show just how important it is to address dangerous misconceptions that are costing lives.

Since 1997 A UN report shows that diagnoses of HIV have increased by 30 per cent each year in Papua New Guinea >>>

1999 A voluntary door-to-door HIV screening programme is set up in Uganda >>>

WHAT THE WORLD THINKS...

These are four different publications commenting on Margaret Marabe's claims that AIDS patients were buried alive in Papua New Guinea. Compare and contrast the various viewpoints and see if you can find any more newspaper reports or other media discussing the investigation.

Daily Telegraph, 31 August 2007

'[Burying relatives alive] is seen as the safest option'. [They believe] if they killed the victims with a machete it would expose them to infection.

Villagers' faith in Western medicine has been eroded in 32 years since independence from Australia by a decline in the public health system. Tribes often lay the blame for Aids on "witches", who are tortured and killed.'

International Herald Tribune, 28 August 2007

'Police and health workers in Papua New Guinea were investigating unverified claims…that people with AIDS were buried alive by their relatives.

"I saw three people with my own eyes," [said Marabe]. "When they got very sick and people could not look after them, they buried them."

…[P]olice and health workers were being sent to the Southern Highlands to investigate the claims…the stigma against people with HIV [is] very strong in the countryside, where education about the disease is scarce.'

Kaiser Daily HIV/AIDS Report, Henry J. Kaiser Family Foundation, 13 September 2007

'The AIDS Committee of Papua New Guinea's Southern Highlands province has found no evidence that people living with HIV/AIDS in the area were buried alive…

The media report sent wrong signals to everyone, including the international community here and abroad, who are funding HIV/AIDS programs in the country.'

The Independent, 28 August 2007

'…[Marabe] said, "Why are they doing that?" And they said, "If we let them live, stay in the same house, eat together and use or share utensils, we will contract the disease and we too might die".'

June 2006 In India, a 15-year-old boy sets himself alight and commits suicide because of the stigma he faces having parents with HIV >>>

December 2006 The WHO predicts that one in five men, women and children in Papua New Guinea will be infected within a decade >>>

Chapter 5

The Battle with AIDS

The fight against AIDS is a global concern, but every country has its own way of dealing with the problem. International organisations try to co-ordinate the effort, but concerted action isn't always easy. Governments have different policies and priorities, situations change, and financial restraints invariably overshadow the good work that is being done.

A worldwide initiative
Statistics show that Africa bears the brunt of the AIDS epidemic. It knows more than any other continent about the real impact of HIV and AIDS. Around 65 per cent of all HIV cases are in sub-Saharan Africa, and almost 90 per cent of children with HIV are living there. But poverty forces these countries to turn to the West for support. Whilst aid and investment are urgently needed, problems arise because supporting countries often have little contact with those most affected.

Access to information
In the Western world, public health campaigns have helped to make a difference. In the early days of the epidemic, blanket media coverage permeated all strands of society and AIDS became a recognised disease very quickly. Sex education programmes began to advise communities, sexual health clinics encouraged HIV testing and offered support, and blood products were screened. But in LEDCs, this transfer of information was not so easily achieved. The limitations of poverty, education and cultural practice simply prevented many public health messages getting through.

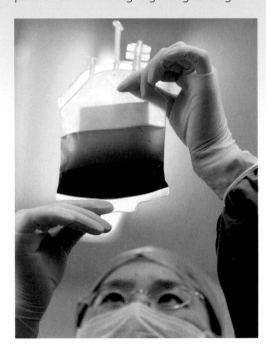

Since 1985, blood products in the Western world have been screened for HIV antibodies and heat-treated to protect patients from infection. This practice is gradually spreading around the world – but in some cases, not soon enough.

Getting the message across
Studies show that in many parts of Africa, community-based sex education is the most effective. While messages need to be conveyed, people also like to take part in the decisions that affect their lives.

In the West, healthcare messages are more readily accepted. But there is now a concern that sex education in schools and mass public awareness campaigns about HIV have declined in recent years. An element of complacency has set in, despite the fact that HIV is as widespread as ever. This rings true particularly in the USA and UK, where, despite additional resources, both homosexual and heterosexual HIV infections are rising. Studies have shown that many young people do not fear catching the deadly disease. This may be because drugs have made the disease less life threatening, or because they have not been faced with alarming publicity campaigns, such as those of the 1980s.

Sex education in African communities is helping to get important messages to a new generation. But resources are limited, and access to support for those living with HIV is proving inadequate.

Effective treatment

Most people with HIV in the Western world have access to treatment, but even then side effects can cause problems of adherence. In LEDCs, only 8 per cent of people living with HIV are currently able to access – and afford – life-saving drugs. In these countries, clean needles are in short supply and inadequate training is causing standards of sterilisation to slip. A lack of proper nutrition is also causing those who have yet to receive medication to develop AIDS very quickly.

1987 An advertising campaign in the UK, 'AIDS: Don't Die of Ignorance', sees leaflets delivered to every household and television adverts warning people about the dangers of HIV >>>

March 1993 South Africa reports that HIV infections are expected to double that year >>>

Routine testing

HIV antibody testing is vital if we are to overcome the AIDS crisis. Studies have shown that less than 1 per cent of the sexually-active urban population in Africa has been tested, for example. And the figure is even lower in rural areas. Free voluntary testing and counselling services are now being offered to help those who cannot pay for health services.

In India, too, mobile HIV counselling and testing units are travelling to remote villages to offer support. In the West, home sampling tests are encouraging more people to take control of their sexual health. But there have been concerns about the accuracy of these tests, and the lack of counselling for those infected.

> **QUOTE >**
>
> Treatments are the key to reducing the impact of HIV, but prevention also relies on people taking control of their sexual health.
>
> 'We shouldn't pretend that we can give injections and work our way out of this. We have to change behaviour, attitudes, and it has to be done in an organized, disciplined, systematic way.'
>
> Former US President **Bill Clinton**, Keynote Address to the National Summit on Africa 17 February 2000.

Microbicides

Microbicides are a method of prevention aimed particularly at women. These gels and creams act like an 'invisible condom' preventing the transmission of HIV during sex. The treatments are designed to enhance the body's natural defences to stop the virus spreading to cells. Microbicides have the potential to save the lives of millions of women who are unable to insist on condom use – these women could use a microbicide without their partner knowing, for example. Microbicides may take up to a decade to develop – they need to be safe, effective, affordable and easy to administer – but these new treatments could revolutionise the prevention of HIV infections.

Alternative treatments

Massage, stress management and herbal remedies are just some of the treatments explored before antiretroviral drugs became available. More recently, vitamin and mineral supplements have been found to stem the virus in some people – a low-cost intervention that could offer hope in the early stages of infection. Other alternative ideas, however, are more alarming. A study of 260 African truck drivers, for example, showed that over a third believed that sleeping with a virgin was one cure for the disease.

In 2006, a scientific study found that male circumcision almost halved the risk of HIV infection among heterosexual men in Africa. This practice may now

 1987 The Soviet Union (USSR) reports its first case of HIV, and tests for the virus are carried out across the country >>>

1992 Scientists explore the first microbicides that could safely prevent the transmission of HIV during sex >>>

26

Although HIV treatments are helping to stem the virus, they are expensive, access may be limited, and side effects are causing problems of adherence. Investment in new technologies, such as vaccines and microbicides, are now offering alternative strategies for the future.

be recommended in many of the countries worst affected by HIV, although cultural beliefs make it an unpopular option for many. There are also concerns that alternative theories of this kind encourage risk-taking behaviour.

Natural immunity?

In 2006, scientists in Boston, USA, began researching findings that some people had a natural resistance to HIV infection. There have been increasing numbers of people living with HIV whose immune system has somehow suppressed the virus so they remain healthy and symptom-free, without treatment. An understanding of how this process works could lead to entirely new drugs in the future.

 November 1999 An early research study claims that male circumcision can help reduce rates of HIV infection in Africa and Asia >>>

Competing priorities

AIDS is life threatening, but in a world where governments have to constantly address conflicting priorities with limited budgets, it's rarely top of the agenda. And in LEDCs, poverty forces other issues, such as education and employment – or basic needs such as drinking water and nutrition – to take priority. Governments also know that AIDS policies are not a natural vote winner, when so many short-term priorities are vying for attention.

Obstructive policies

But when political leaders deny there is an AIDS problem, government inaction goes one step too far. In South Africa, for example, President Mbeki famously claimed that, although HIV could contribute to AIDS, other factors such as

There are now over 3,000 AIDS organisations working worldwide. These groups provide vital education and support to people living with HIV – helping to fill the gap of inadequate government intervention.

poverty and poor nutrition were to blame. South Africans did not have access to antiretroviral treatments until 2003 and the country now has one of the highest rates of HIV in the world. In 2006, more than 11 per cent of South Africa's population had HIV – with estimates that by 2015 over 5.4 million South Africans could die from AIDS.

Denying the risks

For many years, China regarded AIDS as a disease caused by contact with the West. They called it the 'loving capitalism disease' and the government underplayed

 1991 In South Africa, the number of HIV infections among heterosexuals overtakes the number transmitted through homosexual relationships >>>

1997 Brazil is the first LEDC to begin providing free antiretroviral treatment >>>

the severity of the situation. In 1996, 4,500 cases of HIV infection were reported, but in reality China was thought to have up to 100,000 infections.

In 2001, China finally admitted that the AIDS crisis needed addressing. The outbreak of SARS, in 2003, also revealed the dangers of not responding to an emerging epidemic. Public health initiatives have now been set up across the country, but the detention of AIDS activists is confusing the sentiment of the government's efforts.

The impact of China's silence could be huge. Researchers estimate that by 2010, HIV infection in China could increase to between 10 and 20 million. These alarming statistics must be put into context, however – China's population already exceeds 1.3 billion.

Lessons learned

In other countries, government support has seen major success. In 2004, for example, a study revealed that the number of HIV infections in Uganda had fallen from 1.5 million to 0.5 million in a decade, largely thanks to the government's encouragement of health awareness and open communication. Government-sponsored medical research also highlighted the problem, reinforcing messages from the international community. As a result,there was a marked drop in the progression of the epidemic.

AIDS prevention posters such as this one displayed in a Beijing hospital are now widespread in China's cities. But for many years, the government failed to address the problems of HIV.

November 1999 China broadcasts its first television advertisement for condoms in an effort to stop the spread of sexually transmitted diseases and HIV. The advertisement is banned shortly afterwards >>>

Case Study: Thabo Mbeki, the South African president

South Africa is one of the countries most severely affected by AIDS. In 2006, an estimated 5.5 million South Africans were living with HIV, and there were almost 1,000 deaths from AIDS every day.

Slow to respond
While the rest of the world tried to address the challenges of HIV and AIDS through the 1980s and 90s, South Africa failed to provide a serious response to the crisis. The government began to supply antiretroviral treatments in 2003 after intense political pressure – but even then, only a third of patients were receiving treatment by 2007. And almost a third of pregnant women had HIV, giving birth to a new generation of infected children.

The difficulties of a nation
HIV infection in South Africa grew most rapidly at a time when the government was preoccupied with the abolition of apartheid. But when attention finally turned to the AIDS epidemic, intervention measures proved ineffective. The stigma of HIV, often associated as a disease of the poor, meant that many South Africans avoided testing. Women in particular feared physical abuse and a loss of economic security if their partner left them due to their HIV status. And public health

messages were failing to get through to a country that had literacy levels of just 14 per cent, 11 official languages and many isolated rural areas.

Thabo Mbeki's attitudes towards the fight against AIDS have caused outrage in the international community.

Controversial policies
When President Thabo Mbeki spoke at the International AIDS Conference in Durban in 2000, he famously inferred that poverty was the root cause of the epidemic, having worked with scientists who rejected the link between HIV and AIDS. Political pressure grew and in 2006, the government agreed to improve access to treatment. Thankfully, the epidemic is beginning to stabilise – but the effects of inaction have already denied hope to a generation.

October 1987 Dr Peter Duesberg, a US scientist, publishes a report questioning the link between HIV and AIDS >>>

1999 South African President Thabo Mbeki claims the HIV-drug AZT is toxic and could be a danger to health >>>

WHAT THE WORLD THINKS...

These are three different publications commenting on the
plight of AIDS in South Africa and the repercussions of his
views. Compare and contrast the various viewpoints and see
if you can find any more newspaper reports or other media
discussing AIDS in South Africa.

The Daily Herald, Pennsylvania, USA, 18 November 1991

'Scientists cite numerous reasons for the AIDS
plague [in South Africa] including sexual
promiscuity, poor medical services, the
subservient role of women, war and famine.
   Some blacks in South Africa even see
the virus as a plot by whites to preserve
apartheid by persuading blacks to use
condoms, thus reducing the pregnancy rate
in the black population.'

Waterloo Cedar Falls Courier, Iowa, USA, 14 July 2000

'David Ho, one of the world's
leading AIDS researchers, stood
in front of thousands of experts
at the International AIDS
conference and made a statement
that few would have thought
necessary a few months ago:
"HIV is the cause of AIDS"...
Fears President Thabo Mbeki's
recent flirtation with fringe AIDS
theories has...pushed many AIDS
researchers and activists to take a
stand on what has long been
considered a closed issue.
   "Failure to properly address
the modern plague caused by
HIV disease is an act of
irresponsibility that will be
judged harshly by history,"
[said Hoosen Coovadia, the
chair or the International
AIDS Conference in Durban].
"President Mbeki, I beg you not
to allow your legacy to be
defined by inaction on this
human catastrophe."'

European Stars and Stripes, Germany, 26 July 1999

'...[L]ife-extending AIDS drugs
are out of the reach of the average
South African. In a nation that is
grappling with economic
inequalities inherited from the
apartheid regime, per capita GDP
is [US]$4,400 a year. Meanwhile,
name-brand AIDS drugs produced
in Western nations such as the
United States cost as much as
$12,000 a year.'

July 2000 In opposition to Mbeki's views, over 5,000
scientists around the world sign the 'Durban Declaration'
to support the view that HIV is the cause of AIDS >>>

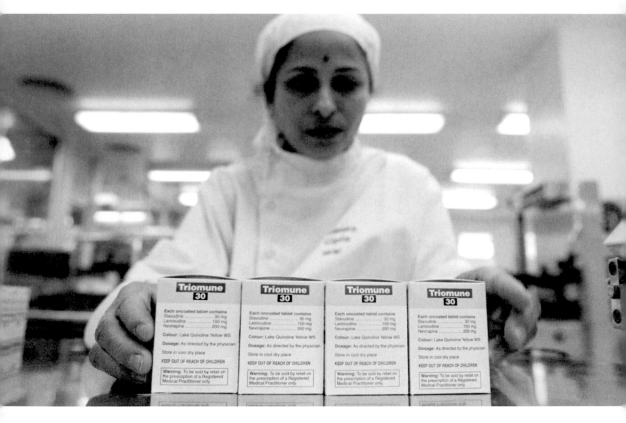

Pharmaceutical profiteering

Pharmaceutical companies have long been accused of cashing in on the fight against AIDS. In 1989, for example, revelations that the drug AZT could slow the progression of HIV saw the value of Burroughs Wellcome, the company behind the drug, rise by 32 per cent. But the cost of AZT remained prohibitive to many – with a year's supply valued at US$7,000. A month later, the company was forced to reduce the cost by 20 per cent.

Pharmaceutical companies claim that treatment costs are high to cover the research and development required to manufacture a drug. However, salaries,

A worker at Cipla's manufacturing outlet packages antiretroviral drugs for the treatment of HIV. The cost of treatment varies from country to country.

publicity and advertising are thought to swallow a large percentage of the profits. Fortunately, the cost of antiretroviral treatments in LEDCs has dropped dramatically in recent years. A year's supply costing several hundred US dollars, can in some places, now be offered for as little as US$148.

Increased competition

An increase in the production of generic drugs is one important contributing factor

 May 2000 Five pharmaceutical companies offer to heavily reduce the price of HIV drugs for Africa and other poor regions >>>

June 2000 The USA offers loans to sub-Saharan African nations to finance the cost of HIV treatments – the offer is rejected by many >>>

to declining costs. In 2001, 39 pharmaceutical companies took the South African government to court for buying cheaper generic HIV drugs from Cipla, a company based in India. But the court case was dropped after intense pressure from international aid agencies who argued that trade laws should not prevent the distribution of life-saving medication. That same year, an international agreement was reached at a World Trade Organisation (WTO) meeting in Doha, Qatar, to make cheap HIV drugs available to all.

But still, controversies over treatment costs continue. In 2007, for example, Cipla was investigated for a 150 per cent price difference between antiretroviral treatments offered to African and Indian buyers. The problem of drug resistance is also a concern. While cheap generic drugs may offer a short-term solution, if strains of HIV become resistant to the drugs, thousands may then be denied access to new, more expensive, medication.

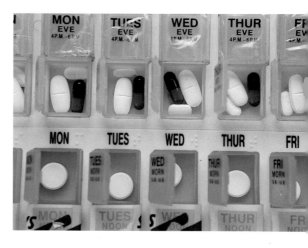

Antiretroviral drugs are developing all the time. These HIV treatments can be taken as three separate pills (top) or a combined pill (below). Generic drugs are much cheaper than their branded counterparts. In 2004, the combined (generic) drug shown here was US$270 per patient per year, while the three separate drugs cost US$560 per patient.

Clinical trials

The only way to test the safety and effectiveness of a drug is to carry out clinical trials. Pre-clinical testing in a laboratory and on animals can determine whether a drug would be effective on humans, but human testing is vital before a drug can go on the market. During these tests, some volunteers are given a placebo so that a comparison can be properly trialled. While there are safety concerns about the drugs being tested, those who are offered a placebo are also putting their lives at risk because they are not being treated.

 2001 Cipla offers cheaper HIV drugs to Medecins Sans Frontieres (MSF). This puts pressure on other pharmaceutical companies to reduce their prices >>>

2001 39 companies halt their court case against the South African government's use of cheaper generic drugs to treat HIV >>>

Case Study: Marty St Clair, who discovered the first HIV treatment

In November 1984, Marty St Clair was running HIV drug trials for her company Burroughs Wellcome when she realised that azidothymidine (AZT) was having an effect against the virus. It was the kind of breakthrough any scientist dreams of. After much painstaking work, she had witnessed the effects of a drug that could reduce the death rate of people around the world.

Hope for the future

Today, it takes up to ten years for a new drug to come on the market, but AZT was made available within three years. People were dying from AIDS, and the world welcomed any drug that might save them.

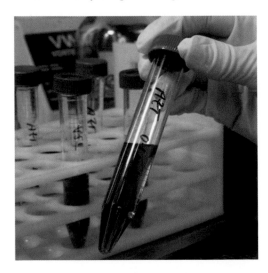

AZT was the first treatment found to have an effect against HIV.

AZT was not a cure for AIDS, but it helped to stem the progression of HIV. It had its drawbacks, however. The drug had severe side effects in some people and within a year many patients began developing resistance to the treatment. But what AZT did achieve, was hope for the future. At last it seemed the effects of HIV could be tackled with science.

Friend or foe?

Despite their continued efforts to find a treatment and cure for HIV, pharmaceutical companies have received a bad press in the 25-year-battle against AIDS. High drug prices, particularly in poorer nations, have brought accusations of profiteering and greed. African nations have even accused Western governments of creating HIV for their own political and financial gain.

There is no doubt that AIDS has brought immense opportunities for pharmaceutical companies to develop their business, but most companies have now agreed to cut the price of their treatments and offer reasons for maintaining appropriate price bands. As HIV continues to spread, indiscriminately, it has also become clear that the burden of AIDS cannot lie solely with the provision of treatments. Attitudes must change, too.

September 1986 Clinical trials show that azidothymidine (AZT) could slow the effects of HIV >>>

1995 A clinical trial proves that a combination of drugs is effective against HIV. The treatment becomes known as Highly Active Antiretroviral Therapy (HAART) >>>

WHAT THE WORLD THINKS...

These are three different publications commenting on AZT and the pharmaceutical industry's role in the fight against AIDS. Compare and contrast the various viewpoints and see if you can find any more newspaper reports or other media discussing HIV treatment.

The Post-Standard, Syracuse, New York, USA, 21 April 2001

"'We are not the Red Cross," [executive vice president of Pfizer Inc] said. *"We are a for-profit company."* In the last year, pharmaceutical companies have slashed the price of AIDS drugs for African countries. In so doing, executives...worry they might be undermining the patents that are the linchpin of their highly profitable industry. And just as frightening is the prospect of activists for other diseases using the AIDS drug offers as a lever to pry out similar concessions. There are other risks – that the drugs will be diverted to a black [illegal] market or that distribution problems in Africa will lead to a stronger strain of the virus.*

Pharmaceutical executives say it's time that other sectors of society took responsibility for the crisis. They note African governments have been slow to respond to their offers and the international community is doing little to build the infrastructure needed to combat the epidemic...There are other issues besides the price of drugs to be addressed."

AllAfrica Global Media website, 29 November 2007

'Clearly...the virus was artificially created to target the Black race in particular. Some researchers...[claim] a cure has been found and is being kept a secret. Instead they promote the use of [antiretroviral drugs] that don't cure AIDS, but instead, earn mountains of money for the pharmaceutical companies.'

BBC News 24 website, 1 December 2007

'There were complaints AZT was expensive and could have toxic side effects. But it offered hope. Not of a cure, but at least of a longer life for [those people] living with [HIV]. [The drug] cost [US]$188 for 100 pills – out of reach for many people. "It was frustrating," Ms St Clair confesses. "But we were doing our very best to make it available as easily as we could."

"I do believe that where you are born shouldn't determine the quality of your health care," said Ms St Clair. "Our company has really made inroads into making drugs available for patients in developing nations."'

Chapter 6

AIDS and the Media

Whatever scientific breakthroughs the future brings, communication is the most important weapon in our fight against HIV and AIDS. And responsible media coverage plays a vital part in this process. While the media can spread educational messages around the globe, it can also relay inaccurate information and reinforce people's prejudices.

The power of the media

The media influences many aspects of our lives, reporting on daily events, shaping people's attitudes, and providing a source of education. In the 1980s, frightening headlines and widespread advertising campaigns attracted the world's attention to AIDS. But today, a new generation is growing up with little knowledge of the disease. Alarmingly, young people (under 25 years of age) now account for half of all new HIV infections worldwide.

Changing headlines

Over the past 25 years, our perceptions of AIDS and HIV have changed dramatically. Once reported as a 'death sentence' and largely a gay problem,

The media plays a vital role in spreading awareness of HIV and AIDS, but sensationalisation can distort the public's perception of the illness.

January 1991 Requests for HIV testing increase in the UK after the character Mark Fowler (from the popular UK soap *Eastenders*) is diagnosed with HIV >>>

November 1991 Freddie Mercury, singer of the rock group Queen, announces he has AIDS just before his death >>>

36

AIDS has now become a 'chronic disease' affecting all walks of life, but one that can be easily managed.

Once in a while, the threat resurfaces, when a celebrity endorses a campaign, when someone famous dies, or when governments are called into question. But as every year goes by, 'AIDS fatigue' brings the risk of the pandemic becoming old news. There is renewed hope, however, that recent interest in international issues, such as the environment and fair trade, will help to bring AIDS the attention it deserves.

In 1987, AIDS awareness in the UK was at its height with a powerful advertising campaign across the country.

QUOTE >

'I think sometimes we think, well, only gay people can get it – it is not going to happen to me. And here I am saying that it can happen to anyone, even me Magic Johnson.'

American basketball player **Earvin (Magic) Johnson**, 'Magic Johnson ends his career, saying he has AIDS infection', *New York Times*, 8 November 1991.

Misunderstandings

Stories that sensationalise the severity of HIV are the most stigmatising of all, widening the divide between those who are, and those who are not, infected. At the other end of the spectrum, a decline in coverage seems to imply that HIV is not an issue any more, perhaps because treatment is now available. The international focus of some reports also encourages people in the West to presume that HIV cannot directly affect them, bringing a danger of complacency.

Use of language

The use of appropriate language is vital when talking about a disease such as AIDS. Misperceptions can be reinforced just by the tone or choice of words used. To describe someone as 'an HIV sufferer', for example, implies that someone living with HIV is helpless and unable to live a full and active life. Our understanding of the causes of infection can also be undermined. To say that 's/he caught HIV' implies that the virus is contagious, even if this was not the sentiment intended.

 1997 AIDS deaths begin to decline in MEDCs, thanks to new drugs >>>   **1999** Heterosexual sex takes over from homosexual sex as the main transmitter of new HIV infections in the UK >>>

37

Case Study: Sarah Porter, prosecuted for reckless HIV transmission

In June 2006, Sarah Porter, a woman from London, was charged with GBH for the 'reckless transmission of HIV'. When an ex-boyfriend complained to the police, an investigation saw Sarah's home raided and her medical records checked. The police tracked down some of Sarah's other sexual partners, and one (who had HIV) filed an official complaint. Sarah was tried and sent to prison for 32 months.

A fair punishment?

Many AIDS organisations oppose the criminalisation of reckless HIV transmission. They say that prosecutions and negative media reports add to the stigma that prevents people being tested for HIV and/or disclosing their HIV status.

Sarah was undoubtedly wrong to hide the fact she had HIV from her sexual partners – and any HIV infection she caused was devastating. But the responsibility of practising safer sex lies with both parties. The first person in a relationship to be diagnosed with HIV is also not necessarily the first to be infected.

When Sarah was first diagnosed, she may not have received the support and advice she needed about disclosing her HIV status to others. Sarah may have been in denial about having HIV, fearing rejection if she told her family and friends.

Bold assumptions

Some media reports implied the case was one of 'deliberate' HIV transmission. Sarah was putting her partners at an extremely high risk, but it is doubtful she wanted to deliberately wreck their lives. Since 2003, there have been a number of prosecutions in England and Wales for the reckless transmission of HIV, under Section 20 of the Offences Against the Person Act 1861. To date, however, there have been no prosecutions of deliberate transmission, which can carry a life sentence.

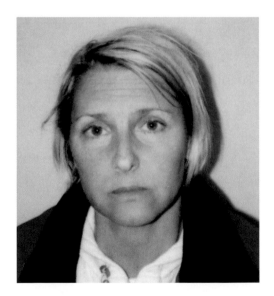

Sarah Porter was one of the first women prosecuted for the reckless transmission of HIV. But were the charges against her fair?

 April 1989 A Dutch man with HIV is jailed in Minnesota under a new law banning people with HIV from entering the USA >>>

1999 A US doctor who injected his former lover with HIV-infected blood is sentenced to 50 years in prison >>>

WHAT THE WORLD THINKS...

These are three different publications commenting on Sarah Porter's conviction in 2006. Compare and contrast the various viewpoints and see if you can find any more newspaper reports or other media discussing the case or the media's reporting of similar prosecutions.

The Sun, 20 June 2006

'A bitter blonde infected with the AIDS virus went on a vengeful mission to spread the disease. Sarah Jane Porter, 43, was made HIV positive by a black lover – and set out to pass it to other Afro-Caribbean men. She is thought to have had unprotected sex with DOZENS. A former lover of Porter told last night how she set out on a callous "payback mission"...[calling her] "sick in the head...She caught HIV off a black guy and now she's on a payback mission. All the guys she has slept with are black... she is a very dangerous woman."'

The Daily Mail, 20 June 2006

'Mr C...added: "Sarah was pure evil in my eyes..." The police have issued an appeal for anyone who may have slept with her since the 1990s. They said that Porter, who has stubbornly refused to name any of her partners, is thought to have had unprotected sex with dozens of men she met at nightclubs in major cities.'

The Independent on Sunday, 22 June 2006

'Detective Sergeant Brian McClusky told journalists that he could not comprehend why Ms Porter had "set about this deliberate chain of events...revenge might have been one possible motive".

The full facts suggest a different picture...The man who turned out to be HIV-positive was...having sex with more than one other woman at the time.

Ms Porter did not insist on unprotected sex on every occasion... She chose, as was her right, to answer "no comment" to all police questions, a fact that has given rise to unfair stories which imply that she refused to help the police to trace her lovers...Her plight is a disaster for everyone working with AIDS.'

 2001 Scotsman Stephen Kelly becomes the first person to be prosecuted in the UK for the reckless transmission of HIV >>>

April 2007 Giovanni Mola, an Italian waiter working in Scotland, is sentenced to nine years in prison for the reckless transmission of HIV and Hepatitis C >>>

Keeping the message alive

With AIDS reports now spanning over a quarter of a century, campaigners need to find new ways to hold the public's interest. With so many other issues clamouring for attention, this can be a struggle. Big-impact stories, such as natural disasters, are prone to grab the headlines, despite the fact that AIDS claims far more lives.

In 1988, the introduction of World AIDS Day helped to redress this balance. Every year on 1 December, an annual themed day helps to raise awareness of HIV and AIDS. This is an opportune time to attract attention, but there is also the risk of high-profile coverage being limited to a single day, and then forgotten.

Access to information

In some countries, public health messages are rarely heard. Cultural taboos about sexuality discourage access to information. Language barriers, illiteracy and the logistics of media channels reaching remote locations are also a problem. But on the positive side, local radio stations with chat shows and phone-ins are proving to be an effective source of information, with an added opportunity for people to get their voices heard.

Films and television programmes, such as *Soul City* – South Africa's most popular

Community media is proving to be a vital tool in the fight against AIDS, with the radio becoming the single most important channel of communication in Africa.

March 1987 ACT UP (the AIDS Coalition to Unleash Power) is founded to campaign for people living with HIV. They hold their first mass demonstration on Wall Street, New York City, USA >>>

1991 The red ribbon becomes an international symbol of AIDS awareness >>>

Members of ACT UP wear masks representing former British Prime Minister Tony Blair (right) and former French President Jacques Chirac (left) as they protest for more AIDS funding during an international conference in Paris.

soap opera, reaching approximately 30 million people across nine African nations – have also helped to spread important messages. The strong AIDS awareness themes in these programmes are making a difference and producers have been inspired to expand this so-called 'edutainment', helped by a US$127 million investment by the US Agency for International Development.

Changing times

With increasing technology, mobile phones, websites, blogs and forums have now joined traditional media channels. This new media is often unchecked, bringing the risk of misrepresentation, but it also provides opportunities for people

living with HIV to access support and advice and to air their views anonymously. When information is spread between communities, messages are also reinforced, giving validity to the information.

Powerful voices

Political activism has also helped to draw the world's attention to the AIDS crisis. South Africa's Treatment Action Campaign (TAC), for example, infamously challenged the government's opposition to antiretroviral drugs. Protests in South African cities (which included threats to bring the dead bodies of activists who had died from AIDS to the demonstrations) were highly publicised around the world, putting intense pressure on the South African government to respond. In the USA too, activist groups such as ACT UP have disrupted AIDS conferences with their protests, adding to high-profile media stories.

 March 1994 The American actor Tom Hanks wins an Oscar for playing a homosexual man with HIV in the film *Philadelphia* >>> | **December 2007** British singer Annie Lennox releases a charity record to raise money and awareness for TAC >>>

Chapter 7

What does the Future Hold?

AIDS has now dominated our lives for over a quarter of a century. Despite a greater understanding of the cause of the disease, and medical advancements in treatment and prevention, we have been unable to stop the pandemic. But there have also been major success stories that give us real hope for the future.

A long-term solution

A continued increase in levels of HIV infection has taught us that the fight against AIDS is a long-term strategy. Governments need to actively support initiatives so that the people most affected are supported and encouraged to change behaviours and attitudes in the long term. And these messages need to be passed to each generation.

AIDS is a global concern, but the most successful interventions have taken place within the context of each country. While we need to learn from each other, every nation also needs to find its own approach to tackling the disease. The response has been most effective in countries with open

These children will have lost many friends and relatives to AIDS. But with the help of the international community, there is hope that their lives could one day be free from HIV.

October 1987 AIDS becomes the first disease to be debated by the United Nations (UN) General Assembly >>>

January 1996 The Joint United Nations Programme on AIDS (UNAIDS) is established >>>

channels of communication, where changes in sexual behaviour are accompanied by a deeper social change. By encouraging public debate, the media can play an important part in challenging established social norms.

How long will it take?

There have been major breakthroughs in the types and cost of treatment, transforming the world's response to HIV and AIDS. But most scientists do not expect a widely available vaccine or cure for the virus within a decade. Instead, it is expected to take at least 20 years to make an impact on the disease.

In the meantime, treatment costs need to be reduced, local healthcare provision requires heavy investment, but, most of all, people need to take responsibility for their sexual health and attitudes must change.

Sustaining activity

In the 1980s, the gay community in the USA mobilised a political response to AIDS, bringing the crisis to the world's attention. More recently, groups such as the TAC have brought changes in Africa, too. This level of public motivation needs to be sustained if governments are to make a difference. In the West, there is a danger that complacency is setting in

> QUOTE >

'In this effort, there is no us and them, no developed and developing countries, no rich and poor – only a common enemy that knows no frontiers and threatens all people.'

Former UN Secretary **General Kofi Annan** at the G8 summit in Genoa, 20 July 2001.

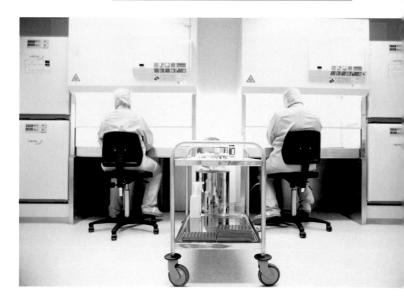

Researchers have been battling with HIV for over 25 years. A cure for the disease is proving difficult to find, but each day we're a step closer to meeting the challenge.

because treatments are beginning to improve the situation. AIDS is a concern for all of us and there is no time to act like the present – whoever we are, and wherever we live.

 May 1997 President Clinton sets a target for the US to find an AIDS vaccine within ten years. This aim is unmet >>>

2004 America launches a major initiative called PEPFAR to combat AIDS worldwide >>>

Case Study: Dr Peter Piot, Executive Director of UNAIDS

On 1 December 2007, the twentieth World AIDS Day saw global campaigns and events drawing attention to the plight of AIDS sufferers. UNAIDS Executive Director Dr Peter Piot urged leaders at all levels of society to hold focus in the battle against HIV, to ensure that positive progress was maintained.

UNAIDS' Dr Peter Piot is leading international efforts in the fight against HIV and AIDS.

A turning point?

Since the first World AIDS Day in 1988, the percentage of the world's population living with HIV has finally stabilised. But there is a long way to go – estimates claim that every day there are more than 6,800 new HIV infections, and over 5,700 deaths to AIDS – alarming statistics.

But at last, the world is beginning to pull together. In 2006, UN member states agreed targets for universal access to HIV prevention, treatment, care and support by 2010. Access to antiretroviral treatment is increasing in sub-Saharan Africa, HIV infections are falling in many countries, and around 30 new vaccines are being tested.

Where do we go from here?

Funding is a major issue for the future. If UN targets on HIV and AIDS are to be achieved by 2010, for example, approximately US$20 billion a year is needed. Issues of stigma and discrimination also need to be tackled urgently to ensure that people take responsibility for their sexual health and complacency is avoided.

In September 2006, the pharmaceutical company Merck stopped human trials of an HIV vaccine because there were worries it might increase the risk of infection to those exposed to the virus. It was a huge blow to the research effort. But while the search for a safe and effective vaccine goes on, improved antiretroviral treatments offer quality of life to those infected and there are renewed hopes that microbicides could soon be available. It's taken more than 25 years, but the victory over AIDS is surely within our grasp.

1 December 1988 The first World AIDS Day takes place. People around the world are urged to 'Join the worldwide effort' >>>

1999 The WHO reports that AIDS has become the fourth biggest killer worldwide >>>

WHAT THE WORLD THINKS...

These are three different publications commenting on World AIDS Day. Compare and contrast the various viewpoints and see if you can find any more newspaper reports or other media discussing the future of AIDS.

**Dr Peter Piot,
UNAIDS press statement,
1 December 2007**

'[A]ccelerating action on AIDS isn't something just for politicians. It involves religious leaders, community, youth and council leaders, chief executives and trade union leaders. It involves people living with HIV, and their families and friends. It involves you, me – each and every one of us – taking the lead to eliminate stigma and discrimination, to advocate for more resources to tackle AIDS. And it requires us all to focus on AIDS every day of the year. '

**Houston Chronicle,
1 December 2007**

'Nowadays...a younger generation has decided that AIDS is not that big a deal, more a treatable chronic illness than a death threat. Such cavalier attitudes risk spreading the disease, catching up new populations in the misery and creating new drains on public health systems.'

**Agence France-Presse,
2 December 2007**

'Activists and global leaders used World AIDS Day on Saturday to warn against complacency in fighting the disease and called on governments to fill a multi-billion-dollar funding gap.

"We have made tangible and remarkable progress on all these fronts. But we must do more," United Nations Secretary General Ban Ki-moon said. "Although global HIV prevalence has levelled off, the numbers are still staggering."

Treatment was still only available to about 10 percent of those in need, [said James Shelton of the US Agency for International Development (USAID)], while in developing countries, "the number of new infections continues to dwarf the numbers who start anti-retroviral therapy in developing countries."'

Agence France-Presse is a global news network based in Paris. It covers events from around the world.

 2001 189 members of the UN sign a Declaration of Commitment on HIV and AIDS pledging to reduce HIV infection among young people (aged 15 to 24) by 25 per cent in the most affected countries by 2005, and to reduce it globally by 25 per cent by 2010 >>>

45

Glossary

ACT UP AIDS Coalition to Unleash Power is a US activist group seeking to end the AIDS crisis. ACT UP protests have brought widespread media attention.

adherence Continuing a course of treatment as prescribed by a doctor, despite difficulties with side effects or methods of application.

anonymous When someone withholds their identity to remain unknown.

antibodies Proteins formed by the immune system to protect the body against foreign substances, such as bacteria and viruses.

antiretroviral Drugs used to treat retrovirus infections, such as HIV.

apartheid A political system in South Africa in the 20th century in which black people were denied basic rights and freedoms.

AZT Azidothymidine is the first antiretroviral treatment found to slow the progression of HIV.

bird flu A type of influenza affecting birds, which has transferred to humans in some cases and has caused death in some parts of Asia.

bisexual A person who is sexually attracted to people of both sexes.

Black Death A type of plague that affected Europe and Asia in the 14th century.

blood transfusion The process of transferring blood from one person to another, for medical reasons.

Caesarean birth An operation used to deliver a baby.

CDC The Centers for Disease Control and Prevention is a US government agency working to promote health and quality of life by preventing and controlling disease, injury and disability.

chronic disease A disease that is long-lasting.

circumcision The surgical removal of the foreskin of the penis for medical or religious reasons.

complacency When people are content, but unaware of the dangers involved.

contagious A disease that can spread from one person to another through surface-to-skin contact or through the air.

discrimination When someone is treated unfairly because they are seen to belong to a particular group.

epidemic A widespread disease.

euthanasia Helping someone to end their life, because they have a terminal illness or an incurable condition.

FDA The Food and Drug Administration is a US government agency working to protect public health by assuring the safety, effectiveness and accessibility of food supplies and medical treatments.

GBH Grievous bodily harm. GBH is an offence that can be prosecuted in a court of law.

generic drug A copy of a brand-name drug that is made by another company at reduced cost.

HAART Highly active antiretroviral therapy. A combination of several (usually three or four) antiretroviral drugs used to treat HIV.

haemophiliac Someone with a genetic disease (usually affecting males) that prevents the blood clotting effectively, to heal wounds.

Hepatitis C A blood-borne infectious disease that infects the liver. Some people with HIV may have contracted Hepatitis C, caused by the Hepatitis C virus (HCV).

heterosexual A person who is sexually attracted to people of the opposite sex.

HIV Human Immunodeficiency Virus is a virus that can lead to AIDS. Two strains of HIV have been identified – HIV-1 and HIV-2. HIV-1 is the cause of most HIV infections, and is more easily transmitted. At the moment, HIV-2 is mainly confined to West Africa.

homophobia Disapproval or discrimination against homosexuals.

homosexual A person who is sexually attracted to people of the same sex.

immune system The way the body protects itself against bacteria, viruses and other infections.

KS Kaposi's Sarcoma is a type of cancer commonly occurring in AIDS patients.

LEDCs Less Economically Developed Countries are the poorer countries of the world, including the countries of Africa, Asia (except Japan), Latin America and the Caribbean.

MEDCs More Economically Developed Countries are the richer countries of the world, including Europe, northern America and Australia.

microbicides Substances used as a barrier to prevent the transmission of viruses.

mutate To change to another form.

pandemic A disease affecting a whole country, or the world.

PCP Pneumocystis carinii pneumonia is a lung infection commonly occurring in AIDS patients.

PEP Post Exposure Prophylaxis is a preventative treatment. PEP is sometimes given after exposure to HIV (or suspected exposure) to decrease the chances of an HIV infection.

pharmaceutical company A company that researches, develops, markets and/or distributes drugs, mostly in the context of healthcare. Examples include: Burroughs Wellcome (the company behind the first antiretroviral treatment for HIV); Cipla (one of the world's largest manufacturers of antiretroviral drugs); Pfizer (one of the world's largest research-based pharmaceutical companies); and GlaxoSmithKline (formed by a series of mergers of Burroughs Wellcome, Glaxo Laboratories, Beecham and SmithKline Beckman).

placebo A substance containing no medication, used as a control during experiments to test the effectiveness of a drug.

racism A belief that people from different parts of the world have different characters or abilities, often leading to discrimination.

SARS A type of virus known as Severe Acute Respiratory Syndrome that began in Asia and the Far East in 2003.

sensationalise To describe something in an extreme way to make it more noticeable.

Spanish flu A severe and deadly form of influenza affecting people around the world in the aftermath of World War I. It received greatest media attention in Spain, hence its name.

stigma A form of prejudice against an individual or a group because they are thought to be different to other people.

sub-Saharan Africa African countries that are found south of the Sahara Desert.

taboo Something that is forbidden because of cultural beliefs.

TAC Treatment Action Campaign is a South African AIDS activist organisation that campaigns for greater access to HIV treatment.

UN The United Nations is an organisation of nations, formed in 1945 to promote peace, security and international co-operation.

vaccination A method of preventing infectious diseases. Vaccinations introduce a bacteria or virus into the body (usually by way of a needle) to encourage the immune system to develop resistance to a disease.

Vatican The papal government, head of the Roman Catholic Church.

WHO The World Health Organisation is the United Nations agency for health.

WTO The World Trade Organisation is an international organisation dealing with the rules of trade between nations.

BOOKS

21st Century Debates: World Health
by Ronan Foley (Wayland, 2002)

At Issue in History: The Discovery of the AIDS Virus
by Lisa Yount (Greenhaven Press, 2003)

Health Issues: AIDS
by Jo Whelan (Wayland, 2001)

Just the Facts: AIDS
by Sean Connolly (Heinemann, 2002)

WEBSITES

African HIV Policy Network
www.aphn.org
Information about the issues faced by Africans living with or affected by HIV.

AVERT
www.avert.org
Facts about HIV and AIDS, including historical timelines and recent news reports.

The Global AIDS Alliance
www.globalaidsalliance.org
A group raising public awareness about the issues affecting those living with HIV and AIDS.

The National AIDS Trust
www.nat.org.uk
Facts about HIV and AIDS, including advice about treatment and prevention.

Terrence Higgins Trust
www.tht.org.uk
Information about HIV and AIDS, from the experiences of those directly affected.

UNAIDS
www.unaids.org
Information about the Joint United Nations Programme on HIV/AIDS.

World AIDS Day
www.worldaidsday.org
Further information about this annual event on 1 December.